"The Customer"
Seminar
8-2-2000

Tim
Kowal

Missy
Shaw
Curt Hollebrands

ATTITUDES

OF

SUCCESS

GWEN WASHINGTON

Glendale Heights, IL 60139

Compiled by Gwen Washington

Cover Design by Design Dynamics
Typeset Design by Julie Otlewis

Published by Great Quotations, Inc.

Library of Congress Catalog Card Number : 98-075790

ISBN: 1-56245-360-2

Printed in Hong Kong

Within the pages of this book

are ideas that can serve as

keystones to building a successful life.

Change your thoughts and you
change your world.

Norman Vincent Peale

Try not to become a man of
success but rather try to become
a man of value.

Albert Einstein

We clothe events with the drapery
of our own thoughts.

James Allen

Do not wait for extraordinary
circumstances to do good;
try to use ordinary situations.

Jean Paul Richter

To think great thoughts you
must be heroes as well
as idealists.

Oliver Wendell Holmes, Jr.

Invest in the human soul.
Who knows, it might be a
diamond in the rough.

Mary McLeod Bethune

You have no right to erect your
toll-gate upon the highways
of thought.

Robert G. Ingersoll

Do something every day that you don't want to do; this is the golden rule for acquiring the habit of doing your duty without pain.

Mark Twain

A man sooner or later discovers
that he is the master-gardener of
his soul, the director of his life.

James Allen

Do not anticipate trouble,
or worry about what may never
happen. Keep in the sunlight.

Benjamin Franklin

How we think shows through in
how we act. Attitudes are
mirrors of the mind.
They reflect thinking.

David Joseph Schwartz

Words are the small change
of thought.

Jules Renard

To be happy, we must not be too
concerned with others.

Albert Camus

Don't compromise yourself.
You are all you've got.

Janis Joplin

Agitation is that part of our
intellectual life where
vitality results; there ideas are
born, breed and bring forth.

George Edward Woodberry

Every man is the architect of his own fortune.

Sallust

Thought is the blossom;
language the bud;
action the fruit behind it.

Ralph Waldo Emerson

Life belongs to the living, and he
who lives must be prepared
for changes.

Goethe

The most powerful factors in the world are clear ideas in the minds of energetic men of goodwill.

J. Arthur Thomson

It is difficult to say what is impossible, for the dream of yesterday is the hope of today and the reality of tomorrow.

Robert H. Goddard

Your belief that you can do the
thing gives your thought
forces their power.

Robert Collier

Language is the blood of the soul
into which thoughts run
and out of which they grow

Oliver Wendell Holmes

What the mind of man can conceive and believe, the mind of man can achieve.

Napoleon Hill

To be persuasive, we must be
believable. To be believable,
we must be credible. To be
credible, we must be truthful.

Edward R. Murrow

Imagination is more important than knowledge.

Albert Einstein

One should examine oneself for a
very long time before
thinking of condemning others.

Moliere

It takes a great deal of elevation
of thought to produce a
very little elevation of life.

Ralph Waldo Emerson

It is hard to fail, but it is worse never to have tried to succeed. In this life we get nothing save by effort.

Theodore Roosevelt

Our thoughts and imaginations
are the only real limits to
our possibilities.

Orison Swett Marden

Believe that life is worth living,
and your belief will help
create the fact.

William James

The actions of men are the
best interpreters of
their thoughts.

John Locke

If two or three persons should
come with a high spiritual
aim and with great powers, the
world would fall into their hands
like a ripe peach.

Ralph Waldo Emerson

Thoughts are energy. And you
can make your world or break
your world by thinking.

Susan Taylor

You are not here merely to make
a living. You are here in
order to enable the world to live
more amply, with greater
vision, with a finer spirit of hope
and achievement. You are
here to enrich the world,
and you impoverish yourself if
you forget the errand.

Little minds are tamed and
subdued by misfortune;
but great minds rise above them.

Washington Irving

If a man harbors any sort of fear,
it percolates through all thinking,
damages his personality and
makes him a landlord to a ghost.

Lloyd Douglas

Think like a man of action and act like a man of thought.

Henri Bergson

Thought makes the whole
dignity of man; therefore
endeavor to think well, that is
the only mortality.

Blaise Pascal

Remember, happiness doesn't depend upon who you are or what you have; it depends solely upon what you think.

Dale Carnegie

Our destiny changes with our thought; we shall become what we wish to become, do what we wish to do, when our habitual thought corresponds with our desire.

Orison Swett Marden

Life loves to be taken by the
lapel and told:
"I am with you kid. Let's go."

Maya Angelou

I think there is only one quality
worse than hardness of heart, and
that is softness of head.

Theodore Roosevelt

There is no thought in any mind,
but it quickly tends to convert
itself into a power, and organizes
a huge instrumentality of means.

Ralph Waldo Emerson

Happiness is found in doing,
not merely in possessing.

Napoleon Hill

Faced with the choice between changing one's mind and proving that there is no need to do so, almost everyone gets busy on the proof.

John Kenneth Galbraith

We are here to add what we can to life, not to get what we can from it.

William Osler

What a thing is to an
unknowable extent is determined
by or influenced by what we
think it is.

Joseph Chilton Pearce

Energy and persistence conquer
all things.

Benjamin Franklin

Our thought is the key which
unlocks the doors of the world.

Samuel McChord Crothers

Everyone thinks of changing the world, but no one thinks of changing himself.

Leo Tolstoi

If you can imagine it, you can achieve it. If you can dream it, you can become it.

William Arthur Ward

Impossibility: a word only
to be found in the dictionary
of fools.

Napoleon Bonaparte

We never do anything well till
we cease to think about the
manner of doing it.

William Hazlitt

You can't have a better tomorrow
if you are thinking about
yesterday all the time.

Charles F. Kettering

There are glimpses of heaven to
us in every act, or thought,
or word, that raises us
above ourselves.

Arthur P. Stanley

Failures are divided into two
classes - those who thought
and never did, and those who did
and never thought.

John Charles Salak

You must do one thing you think
you cannot do.

Eleanor Roosevelt

What you do speaks so loud that
I cannot hear what you say.

Ralph Waldo Emerson

Where all men think alike, no
one thinks very much.

Walter Lippmann

Every thought seed sown or
allowed to fall into the mind, and
to take root there, produces its
own, blossoming sooner or later
into act, and bearing its own
fruitage of opportunity
and circumstance.

James Allen

Destiny is no matter of chance.
It is a matter of choice;
it is not a thing to be waited for,
it is a thing to be achieved.

William Jennings Bryan

A man's life is what his thoughts make it.

Marcus Aurelius

Certain thoughts are praye
There are moments when
whatever be the attitude (
body, the soul is on its k

Victor Hugo

We must learn to live together as
brothers or perish together
as fools.

Martin Luther King, Jr.

Let us train our minds to desire
what the situation demands.

Seneca

The best portion of a good man's life
is his little, nameless unremembered
acts of kindness and of love.

William Wordsworth

Every good thought you think is
contributing its share to
the ultimate result of your life.

Grenville Kleiser

There are no limitations to the
mind except those we
acknowledge. Both poverty and
riches are the offspring
of thought.

Napoleon Hill

We can control our thoughts...
and by controlling our thoughts...
by using this greatest power...
the power to choose...
we are indirectly able to
control conditions.

J. Martin Kohe

Every human mind is a great
slumbering power until awakened
by a keen desire and by definite
resolution to do.

Edgar F. Roberts

Men are disturbed, not by the things that happen, but by their opinion of the things that happen.

Epictetus

Ideals are like stars:
we never reach them, but like the
mariners of the sea, we chart our
course by them.

Carl Schurz

Creative minds have always been
known to survive any kind of
bad training.

Anna Freud

At a certain age some people's minds close up; they live on intellectual fat.

William Lyon Phelps

High aims form high characters,
and great objects bring out
great minds.

Tryon Edwards

All that you are is a result of all
that you have thought.

Buddha

Positive anything is better than negative nothing.

Elbert Hubbard

Other Titles by Great Quotations, Inc

Hard Covers

African American Excellence

Ancient Echoes

Attitudes of Success

Behold the Golfer

Celebrating Friendship

Commanders In Chief

Dare to Dream

First Ladies

Graduation

Golf

Good Lies for Ladies

Heartfelt Affection

Improving With Age

Inspirations for Success

Inspired Thoughts

I Thought of You Today

Journey to Success

Just Between Friends

Keys to Achieving Your Goals

Lasting Impressions

My Dear Mom

My Husband, My Love

Never Ever Give Up

Peace Be With You

Seeds of Inspiration

Seeds of Knowledge

Sharing Our Love

Sharing the Season

Smile Now

Teddy Bears

The Essence of Music

The Passion of Chocolate

The Perfect Brew

The Power of Inspiration

There's No Place Like Home

The Spirit of Christmas

Thoughts From Great Women

Great Quotations, Inc.
1967 Quincy Court
Glendale Heights, IL 60139 USA
Phone: 630-582-2800 Fax: 630-582-2813
http://www. greatquotations.com

Other Titles by Great Quotations, Inc

Paperbacks

A Servant's Heart
A Teacher is Better Than Two Books
I'm Not Over the Hill
Life's Lessons
Looking for Mr. Right
Midwest Wisdom
Mommy & Me
Mother, I Love You
Motivating Quotes
Mrs. Murphy's Laws
Mrs. Webster's Dictionary
Only A Sister
Parenting 101
Pink Power
Romantic Rhapsody
Social Disgraces
Stress or Sanity
The Mother Load
The Other Species
The Secret Langauge of Men
The Secret Langauge of Women
The Secrets in Your Name
Teenage of Insanity
Touch of Friendship
Wedding Wonders
Words From the Coach

Perpetual Calendars

365 Reasons to Eat Chocolate
All Star Quotes
Always Remember Who Loves You
A Touch of Kindness
Coffee Breaks
Extraordinary Leaders
Generations
I'm a Little Stressed
I Think My Teacher Sleeps at School
Kid Stuff
My Friend & Me
Never Never Give Up
Older Than Dirt
Secrets of a Successful Mom
Shopoholic
Sweet Dreams
Teacher Zone
Tee Times
The Dog Ate My Car Keys
The Essence of Great Women
The Heart That Loves
The Honey Jar
Winning Words

Destiny is no matter of chance.
It is a matter of choice;
it is not a thing to be waited for,
it is a thing to be achieved.

William Jennings Bryan

A man's life is what his thoughts make it.

Marcus Aurelius

Certain thoughts are prayers.
There are moments when
whatever be the attitude of the
body, the soul is on its knees.

Victor Hugo

Every thought seed sown or
allowed to fall into the mind, and
to take root there, produces its
own, blossoming sooner or later
into act, and bearing its own
fruitage of opportunity
and circumstance.

James Allen

Other Titles by Great Quotations, Inc

Hard Covers

African American Excellence

Ancient Echoes

Attitudes of Success

Behold the Golfer

Celebrating Friendship

Commanders In Chief

Dare to Dream

First Ladies

Graduation

Golf

Good Lies for Ladies

Heartfelt Affection

Improving With Age

Inspirations for Success

Inspired Thoughts

I Thought of You Today

Journey to Success

Just Between Friends

Keys to Achieving Your Goals

Lasting Impressions

My Dear Mom

My Husband, My Love

Never Ever Give Up

Peace Be With You

Seeds of Inspiration

Seeds of Knowledge

Sharing Our Love

Sharing the Season

Smile Now

Teddy Bears

The Essence of Music

The Passion of Chocolate

The Perfect Brew

The Power of Inspiration

There's No Place Like Home

The Spirit of Christmas

Thoughts From Great Women

Great Quotations, Inc.
1967 Quincy Court
Glendale Heights, IL 60139 USA
Phone: 630-582-2800 Fax: 630-582-2813
http://www. greatquotations.com

Other Titles by Great Quotations, Inc

Paperbacks

A Servant's Heart
A Teacher is Better Than Two Books
I'm Not Over the Hill
Life's Lessons
Looking for Mr. Right
Midwest Wisdom
Mommy & Me
Mother, I Love You
Motivating Quotes
Mrs. Murphy's Laws
Mrs. Webster's Dictionary
Only A Sister
Parenting 101
Pink Power
Romantic Rhapsody
Social Disgraces
Stress or Sanity
The Mother Load
The Other Species
The Secret Langauge of Men
The Secret Langauge of Women
The Secrets in Your Name
Teenage of Insanity
Touch of Friendship
Wedding Wonders
Words From the Coach

Perpetual Calendars

365 Reasons to Eat Chocolate
All Star Quotes
Always Remember Who Loves You
A Touch of Kindness
Coffee Breaks
Extraordinary Leaders
Generations
I'm a Little Stressed
I Think My Teacher Sleeps at School
Kid Stuff
My Friend & Me
Never Never Give Up
Older Than Dirt
Secrets of a Successful Mom
Shopoholic
Sweet Dreams
Teacher Zone
Tee Times
The Dog Ate My Car Keys
The Essence of Great Women
The Heart That Loves
The Honey Jar
Winning Words